BREWING

FOR

BEER-GINNERS

A simple guide to making beer from kits and brewing with grains and hops

by Gary Mottram

All content © Gary Mottram 2014

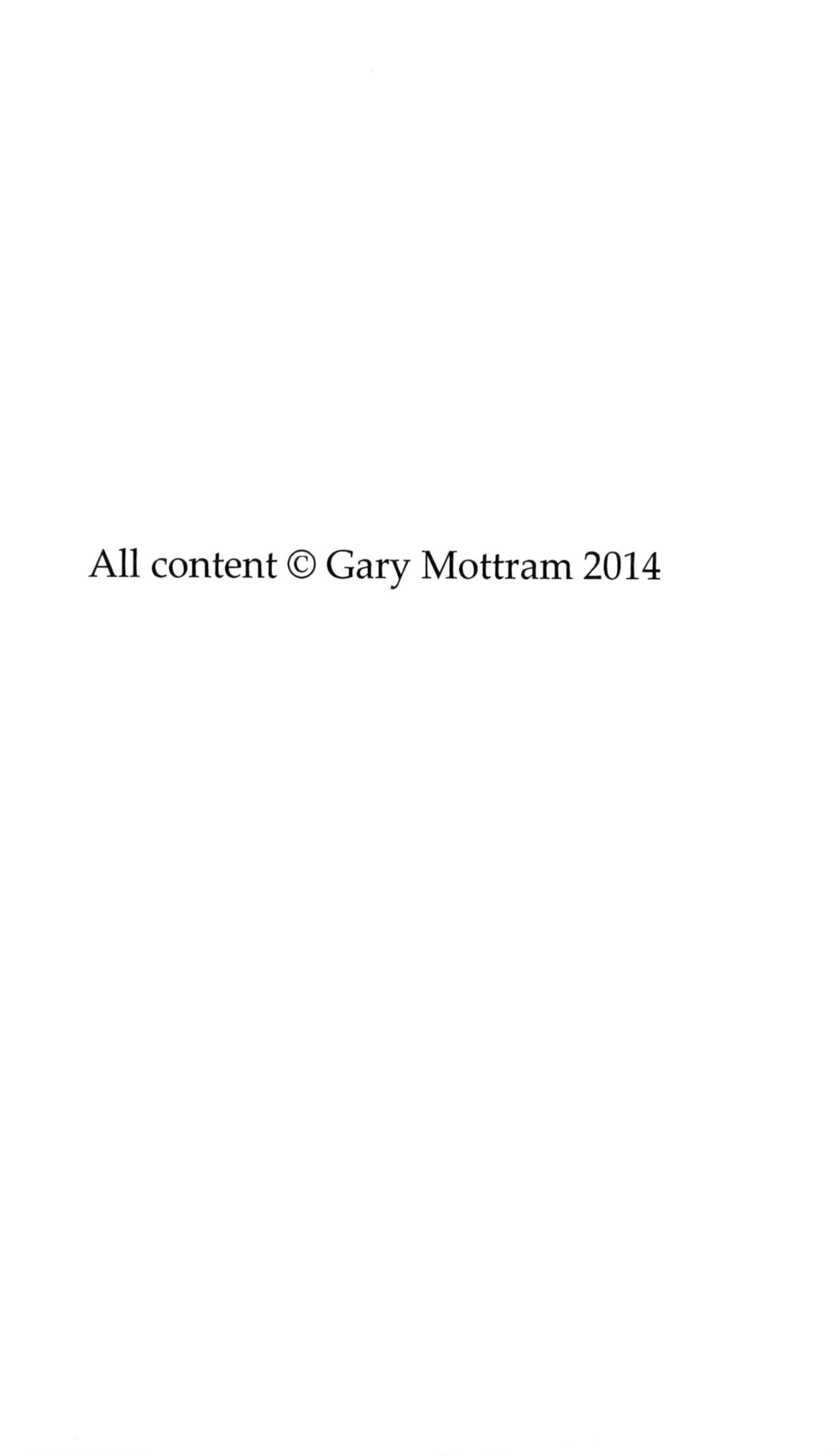

About This Book	7
Introduction	10
Making Beer From A Kit	23
The Hydrometer	30
Let's Brew	38
How To Brew All Grain Beer	47
-The Process	51
-The Mash	52
-The Sparge	53
-The Boil	55
-Equipment	58
Pre-Brew	65
-Test Your Gear	66
-Water Volume	68
Let's Brew Some AG	72
-Efficiency	87
-Mash Temperature	89
How Much Does It Cost?	91
Useful Links	96

About This Book

This book will help you in your first foray into brewing beer.

It wasn't that long ago that I was getting the equipment together and reading up on all grain brewing myself, so all the language will be easy to understand and well-explained, with pictures where necessary. This book will help to explain equipment you will need and how to use it. It will also give you some recipe ideas so you can make a decent pint of beer.

Remember, this hobby is supposed to be fun so don't stress about things too much, don't panic, and don't worry too much about hitting targets. You can worry about all that stuff later on once you have had hands-on experience of brewing.

It does pay to be prepared though and keeping this book handy, as well making a list of all the processes, weights, volumes and temperatures you need, will certainly be of benefit.

Beer is very forgiving and it is well worth remembering that it has been brewed for centuries without the need for any qualifications, chemical knowledge or analysis. The average homebrewer does not need to know much more than the ingredients to use for beer, the steps involved and the ideal conditions for fermentation, much like a cook needs to know the ingredients and instructions to make bread, without having to know why the yeast makes it rise or what chemical reaction is occurring within.

One may, out of interest, wish to gain additional knowledge of the vast subject that is 'brewing' as it is very interesting and some aspects will be useful in the future. Just for now though, it is not really necessary and it is best not to get too bogged down in it.

Given the correct conditions, beer will be made.

As is mentioned elsewhere in this book, everything should be kept clean and sterilised as in the same conditions that yeast thrives, so do other forms of bacteria which can harm your brew and will, almost certainly, result in the whole lot having to be tipped down the drain. Considering the time, effort, and costs involved, this is best avoided.

If the worst does happen though, learn by your mistakes and do better with your next brew!

Introduction

The first beer I produced was a kit beer. I had watched my father make wine, gallons and gallons of wine, from apples to elderberries, oranges to wheat. I will always remember the 'blup blup' sound from the airlocks in the demijohns which were on the shelf of our garden shed. When I left for my paper round at 6 in the morning, when I arrived home from school in the evening, when I went out to play at the weekend; 'blup blup' was the soundtrack.

My sisters and I were always drafted in to help pick ripe fruit or fresh flowers from the trees that we would be driven to, Tupperware boxes on our laps for the pickings, on a sunny Sunday afternoon. Of course, as a sort of repayment for our hard work, we were allowed a glass or two with our dinner. I can still taste the sweetness of the elderflower wine, the bite of the rhubarb wine, the aroma of rose petal wine. The wine never seemed to run out either. I'm not sure how much wine my dad actually made but it seemed like he had a small production plant going, although I never really remember him actually bottling wine or cleaning out demijohns so maybe it was all taken care of late at night or when we were out.

He wasn't the only one at it. Most of my uncles had made wine or beer at some point, as had a lot of family friends, all with varying degrees of success. There was one uncle that made carrot 'whisky' and actually added a bottle of whisky to the wine. He didn't scrape or clean the carrots either, and I clearly remember the layer of scum that was floating along the top. I am not sure whether it was actually drinkable but he did live to make potato 'whisky', his next brew, complete with a piece of toast spread with yeast floating on the top. Then there was the neighbour that gave my dad a gallon of cider. Proper cider from apples. He had lovingly created a cider press (or apple press) and had used the apples from the three trees in his garden. My dad, on spying the layer of scum on top of the liquid, placed it in the shed out of sight. A week later, large clumps of mould had formed on the scum and, I could be wrong but I'm sure I'm not, the whole lot went down the sink. There was another uncle of mine that came over to our house one night. He proclaimed himself as a bit of a drinker and enjoyed a few of my dad's more delicate homemade wines. It all went badly wrong when my dad brought out a bottle of wheat wine. A couple of glasses of that finished my uncle off and he had to be driven home by my auntie. In airing cupboards and garden sheds up and down the country, yeast was turning sugar into alcohol and CO_2 on an industrial scale. The making and selling of alcohol had been strictly regulated, even for small scale homebrewers, up until 1963, when the law was changed and, thankfully, this still stands today.

Home wine and beer makers can make alcohol in any quantity, at any strength, without paying duty, as long as it is not sold and is for personal consumption.

When I started working, I wanted to make beer. The conversation had arisen in the work's canteen one day.

Some would say "It'll blow your head off!"

"I never had any luck with it, I think I drank it too early" others would say, regretfully.

This was back in the time when every town had its own homebrew shop. These shops had a wide array of beer kits, wine kits, and everything the budding home brewer would need to get started in this fantastic hobby. Most of these shops are sadly gone, only a few lucky people will still smell that beautiful aroma that would hit you upon entering these establishments, and have all that choice of beer kits and ingredients. Imagine all the beer, wine and cider kits that you can buy on eBay, all in one place. That's maybe a slight exaggeration, but not too far from the truth.

I broached the subject to my dad, and he was all for showing me how to make up beer from a kit. He also told me that, when he was a younger man, he had made 'proper' beer, from grains and hops, boiling the wort, and making different recipes. This didn't really appeal to me back then, I was just a 17 year old that wanted to make some cheap booze. I really wish I had quizzed him further on the subject but, alas, never did.

In my next lunch break, I headed into town and purchased my first beer kit: EDME Superbrew Bitter. It contained hopped malt extract and yeast. Just add sugar and water.

My dad showed me how to make the kit up that weekend. It all looked fairly easy; Heat extract tin so it flows easily, pour into sterilised fermenting bin, fill with water, add sugar, wait until it's cooled to room temperature, sprinkle yeast on, stick in airing cupboard and wait.

It took about a week for the bubbles to stop and we transferred the beer into an old pressure keg that my dad had in the garage (cleaned and sterilised first, of course). He reckoned it would be a week or two before we'd be able to drink it. Then the day arrived, it was summer and I was sat in the kitchen. My dad had been digging his vegetable plot in the garden and was sweating away, and probably very thirsty, so he decided the time was right to 'test' the beer. Glasses at the ready, we pulled off a glass each from the barrel. Ah, refreshing. I can still remember the taste of that first homemade beer. Anyway, we enjoyed the first beer, so had another. All I remember was my dad, standing at the back door, announcing that he felt a bit drunk! He was never really one for drinking, and certainly not getting drunk (except in his younger years) and this had me in hysterics. I can only think the beer went straight to his head in the summer heat.

Back at work, one of the 'experts' on beer told me that you could drink it sooner as, if you look around the homebrew shop, you can find many powders and potions to add to beer to make it clear quicker and be drinkable earlier. I told my dad about this (the idea sounded good to me) and he said that if you were going to add loads of chemicals to beer, you might as well go and buy commercially-produced beer and, if you have a bit of patience with your home-made ale, it will be ready when it's ready and all the better for it. Good point. I have stuck by this ever since and never use finings, flavour enhancers or chemicals of any description in either beer or wine.

After the initial beer kit, I think we made one more and it somehow fizzled out and, for some reason, it took nearly 20 years for me to make another. It had always been in the back of my head as being something I'd like to try again, but I just never got round to it. A year or so after my dad died, my mum was clearing out the shed and phoned me to ask if I wanted any of his old brewing and wine making equipment. I said no as I couldn't see myself getting round to using it, and didn't really have much room for it in the house. She couldn't give it away so ended up recycling most of it and dumping the rest.

I'm not sure how or why I started again. I just had the urge to make alcohol. I ordered a starter homebrew kit from the internet which came with everything you would need to start making beer including a 5 gallon fermenting bin, Lager beer kit, syphon tubes, yeast etc. The only thing missing was bottles but I had been saving up my empties for a while for the recycling bin, so had a good stash of them in the shed. I made the kit up and left it to ferment. I had chosen lager as I thought it would be a nice drink and one of the easiest to make successfully. I was wrong. Lager is one of the harder drinks to make as it needs to be fermented at a lower temperature than beer (about 10° to 12° Celsius for lager, 18° to 22° for ales) and would take much longer to finish. It would also need to be stored (lagered) for a few weeks (or longer) before bottling. Oh well, you live and learn. I bottled the beer, priming each bottle with a bit of sugar, left it for a week in a warm place, then into a cool place for another week, then it was ready to drink. It was a bit bland, had no fizz whatsoever, no real body, but it did contain alcohol, evident after drinking three or four pints. It wasn't perfect, but I had successfully made alcohol of my own. I believe every man and woman should at least once, a kind of rite of passage.

After this, I experimented with various 'turbo' drinks (cider made from supermarket apple juice, add some sugar, ferment) and experimented with a whole different array of flavours. None of them were particularly good, but they all made alcohol and were all drinkable.

By now, I was bitten by the bug. I spotted an advert in the local paper, someone was selling some one gallon demijohns. I paid the man £10 for 5. He had about 20 for sale, plus a fruit press and various other odds and ends, but I didn't think I'd need any more than 5. About a week later, I regretted not buying everything he had, including the press. I got hold of a few books on wine making and started collecting fruit and flowers, just like we had as kids for my dad. I then found a shop not too far away that had a homebrew section. They had about 10 different beer kits plus bottles, sterilising powder, corks, bottle caps, everything you needed to get started. I purchased a kit (EDME Bitter again) and set it fermenting. I also found a couple of 'King Keg' pressure barrels online that I snapped up, the idea being that while I was drinking from one, I could fill the other and leave it to mature. Drinking beer too early is a big problem for homebrewers and, though it is good to taste beer at various times as it is helpful to taste the different stages of maturation, it is not good to drink all the beer before it has reached its prime. For some beers, this can be 2 weeks, for other beers (usually a heavy beer such as stout) it can take months to reach its best.

I have made many kits from cheap ones to the more expensive 'all extract' kits (those that don't require the addition of sugar) and some are great, some not so good. Very early on, I discovered that if you add spraymalt instead of sugar, added 'like for like' (1kg sugar = 1kg spraymalt) it will give your beer better body and a more rounded flavour. Once I started doing this, I never went back to adding sugar. Some people add hops to their kit beers. Some kits, usually the expensive ones, have a 'tea bag' that contains hops and is added to the fermentation to add a bit of extra hop flavour and aroma. Another trick with beer kits is to only make them to 30 pints, instead of 40. This will produce a stronger beer with a fuller body.

The next stage of the process is to make beer from malt extract, complete with 60 minute boil and hop additions. This is the midway point between kits and all grain as it combines both processes and is still easier than doing a full mash. I skipped this step though and it is not covered by this book. I went straight from kits to all grain…..

I used to read books on brewing all grain beer (from now on known as AG) but decided it looked too difficult, too time consuming, and expensive to start up. It was a chain of processes that I just couldn't get my head around.

AG brewing is making beer from the four ingredients;

Water

Malt

Hops

Yeast

Then, I started to look around the internet for advice on the various stages of brewing and things started to 'click' in my head. The process of boiling and fermenting I understood, but what was 'Mashing'? 'Sparging'?

All will be explained in very simple terms in the chapter 'How To Brew All Grain Beer' But first, you may wish to get the gear together to start making kits, as a good way of learning a bit more about the process. The gear will still be usable if you decide to start AG brewing and it will mean slightly less to buy when the time comes.

Making Beer From A Kit

To start making beer from a kit, you will need the following equipment;

5 gallon fermentation bucket with lid

Syphon Tube

Sterilising Powder

Beer kit of your choice (should come with yeast)

Sugar (or spraymalt)

Bottles (+ bottle caps and capper) **or pressure barrel**

Fermenting Bucket

This must be food grade plastic, any good homebrew stockist will sell them. 5 gallons is a good size to start with. This will easily hold 40 pints of beer, which most kits make. There is usually a 5 gallon/40 pint mark on the outside of the bucket so you know where to fill the water to and, if there's not, it is well worth getting a measuring jug and filling it with 40 pints of water and marking off where the level is. It can also be worth marking off the 10/20/30 pint marks too.

Sterilising Powder

This is one of the most important aspects of brewing, whether AG, kit, wine or cider;

EVERYTHING MUST BE CLEAN

Anything that your beer will touch, or anything that will touch your beer, must be sterilised. I use V.W.P. powder for this purpose as it's quick to work, easy to rinse, and doesn't leave any smell, unlike some other brands. It's all down to personal choice and what you have available to you, though. Any spoon, fermenting vessel, thermometer, must be sterilised first. I draw the line at sterilising my hands but do know of people that do. A good wash with soap and water will be fine.

Syphon Tube

This will be needed to transfer the finished beer from the fermenter to either your pressure barrel or bottles. Ideally, it will have a tap at one end. This will ensure that you have control over the flow of beer and is more useful for bottling than when transferring to a pressure barrel.

Beer Kit

Take your pick! Real ale, bitter, stout, lager, dark ale, blond ale, light ale, mild, IPA, porter, they are all available, plus more. I would pick a style of beer that you like to drink but, as I said previously, would probably steer clear of lager to start with.

Sugar or Spraymalt

1 kg of sugar from your supermarket will do. If you're feeling a little more adventurous, buy a kilo of spraymalt from your chosen homebrew supplier. I personally go for spraymalt as it does make quite a big difference to the finished beer, though does add a few more quid to the overall price. It is available in Light, Medium or Dark, so choose the colour which will suit your beer best.

Bottles or Pressure Barrel

Bottles are free and easy to get hold of (just make sure they were used for beer in the past and will hold the pressure as you don't want them exploding beer and shards of glass everywhere). Real ale bottles such as those you can buy at the supermarket will do and brown bottles. 500ml (1 Pint) bottles are better than smaller bottles as it takes longer to clean and fill 330ml bottles. If that's all you can get hold of, they will do the job. You will also need some bottle/crown caps and a crown capper to enable you to seal the bottles. If you are lucky enough to find 40 flip-top bottles (Grolsch etc) snap them up as they will save you a lot of time and money.

If you are serious about investing money in brewing, a pressure barrel might be for you. They are easy to fill, easy to clean, and it is extremely satisfying to pull a pint of your own draught beer. They vary in price though and will need to have a pressure release valve on the lid. This will allow any excess pressure inside the barrel to escape, whilst also allowing you to pressurise the barrel with CO_2 as, once some of the beer has been drunk and the level is low, the pressure will drop and the beer will stop running from the tap. There are top and bottom tap versions available, the advantage of a top tap being that less time has to pass to get clear beer into your glass.

Other items you may find useful;

Thermometer

Hydrometer

Fermentation heater

Large pot or saucepan

Thermometer

The temperature of beer is very important at certain stages, namely fermentation and pitching the yeast. Fermentation for ales (but not lager) should ideally be somewhere between 18° and 21° Celsius. Room temperature will do, just make sure the fermenter doesn't get too hot as this will give the finished beer off flavours, and if it gets too cold, the yeast may stop working and the fermentation will stop. An even temperature in an unheated spare room may do the trick, though check with your thermometer first. It is not so important to use a thermometer for making beer kits, but one will be absolutely necessary once you start making all-grain beer.

Hydrometer

This is used to measure the amount of sugar in the wort (unfermented beer). Taken before fermentation starts (known as original gravity or OG), this measurement can be used to determine how much alcohol (%ABV) will be in the finished beer. As the yeast eats away at the sugar, turning it to alcohol, the gravity will drop (known as attenuation) and, once all the yeast has turned as much sugar as it is going to into alcohol, a final reading can be taken (final gravity or FG) which determines the amount of alcohol in the beer. If the reading remains the same over three days, the beer has finished and can safely be bottled. The temperature of the liquid you are measuring plays a part and, to take an accurate reading, it should be 20°C. This is what most hydrometers are calibrated to. Again, I never used a hydrometer when making kit beers just because it seemed like a hassle. It is well worth getting to grips with it at an early stage though, as it becomes a must-have item, once you start AG brewing and will become an essential part of your kit. They are cheap so buy two as you will inevitably break one at some point. It is also worth buying a sample tube, either glass or plastic, so you can measure the liquid with ease.

Reading The Hydrometer

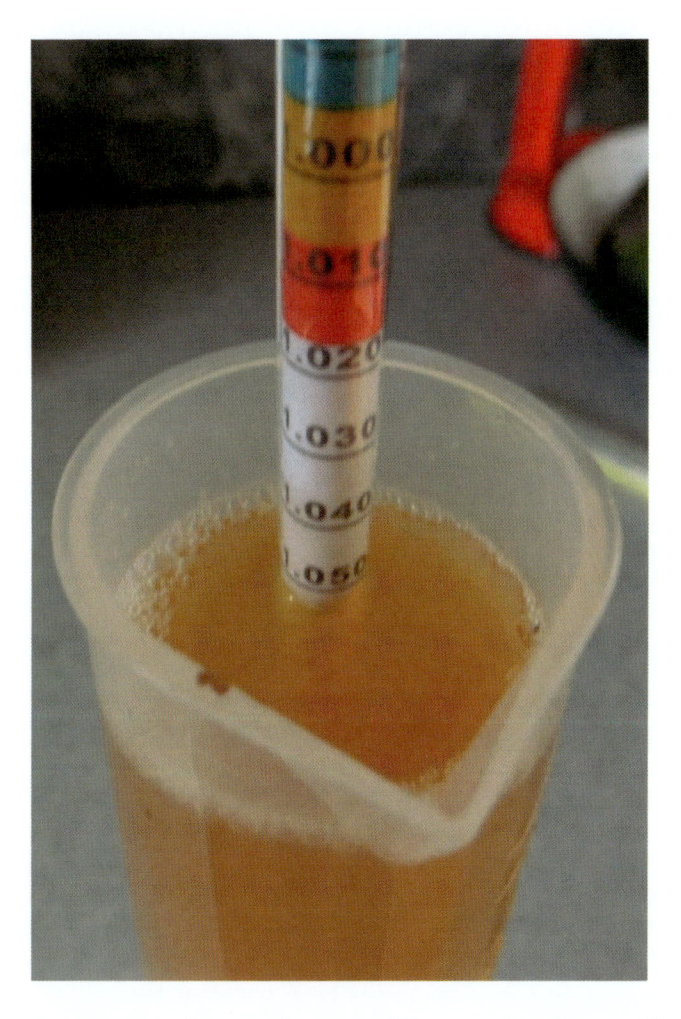

In the image above, the specific gravity is reading 1.054

It is essential to read the hydrometer properly and this can only be done by having the level of the liquid at eye level. The water will 'bulge' up around the glass tube giving a false reading.

The correct reading is obtained by the method below;

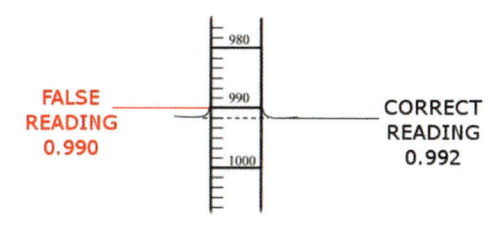

FALSE READING 0.990

CORRECT READING 0.992

The hydrometer will have a numbered scale on the side, usually ranging from 0.990 at the top to 1.120 at the lower end. When placed in water, assuming it's 20° C, the reading should be 1.000. Add some sugar to the water and the water will become denser, so the reading will rise. Ferment that sugar and the liquid will become lighter, so the reading will drop. Beer will usually finish somewhere between 1.010 and 1.006. Some wines will finish at 0.998 or lower due to higher alcohol and it being less dense than water.

Most Hydrometers are calibrated to 20°C so it is important to wait for the liquid to cool to this temperature, or to adjust the figure using your brewing software (calculators can also be found online). There is a formula to work this out but I have found it to be so complicated that it is not worth the effort when there are so many good calculators that will do the sums for you.

Using a Hydrometer probably sounds complicated to a beginner, I know it did to me when I first started out, but it is easy enough and will come with a bit of practice. Study the scale, test it in water, add some sugar to see the effect, and use it every time you brew a batch of beer.

Fermentation Heater

This isn't strictly necessary if you have somewhere to keep your fermenting beer at the correct temperature. I have recently purchased a couple of aquarium heaters as, living in a cooler part of the country, the temperature is often low here, even in summer, and especially during the night. I can either plonk the heater straight into the beer (making sure it is clean and sterilised first) or, my chosen method, stand the fermentation bucket in a bath of water and place the heater in the water. This is less hassle as it means less chance of infecting the beer and less work as I don't have to make sure the heater is clean each time. The bath is an old recycling box, like the ones used at the kerbside for newspaper and food tin collections, which I have lined with a heavy duty plastic bag to avoid leaks. Some beer, when rapidly fermenting, can overflow the lid and end up all over the place. Be aware of this if you are fermenting in your spare room or a corner of the living room as it will make a very sticky mess on the carpet. This is another reason why I use a heater as all my fermentation takes place in a dedicated 'brew shed', complete with concrete floor, which can easily be hosed down in the event of a mishap (and there have been a few!).

Large Pot or Saucepan

This isn't strictly needed but does come in handy when making kits as the tin of extract can be stood in hot water for 10 minutes or so, making it nice and fluid to work with. If you try and pour it cool, it will be like the thickest treacle you have ever seen and either not budge, or take ages to pour. If heated, just remember that the tin will be hot so use a tea towel or oven gloves! A large saucepan can also be handy for filling the near-empty tin with hot water to get all of the extract out but you may find a kettle will do the job just as well. I have a large 'berry pan' for standing the extract can in, and an old pressure cooker for heating water in. Both items came from a charity shop and didn't cost more than a couple of quid.

So, assuming you now have all of the above kit together, or just the essentials you need, let's get started…….

Let's Brew

- Rinse out your fermentation bucket with cold water. Twice.

- Fill it with warm water and add the recommended dose of your chosen sterilising/sanitising powder, giving it a stir with your hand. Get some on the lid too, and drop anything else that you will be using into the bucket.

- Open the plastic lid from the top of the beer kit and remove the instructions and yeast, put them safely aside.

- Get a tin opener and open the lid of the beer kit.

- Place the beer kit tin into some warm water, to loosen the extract.

- Rinse out your fermenting bin with cold water. Twice. Until there is no trace of any foam or suds left over. Make sure that whatever else was in the bucket is put somewhere clean and safe.

- Put a full kettle, or a full large saucepan of water, on to boil.

- Empty the contents of the tin into your bucket.

- Add sugar or spraymalt* to the bucket now.

*It is much easier to add spraymalt to the fermenting bucket BEFORE adding hot water, as *the steam will cause the spraymalt to get damp and stick together in the packet so it will be difficult to pour*

- Rinse the tin out two or three times with hot water, sloshing it round to get all of the malt extract out.

- Add some hot water to a glass and leave to cool and, once at room temperature, sprinkle in the yeast. Leave aside.

- Add more hot water to the fermenting bin and stir with a (sterilised) spoon to dissolve the malt and sugar/spraymalt.

- Fill the bucket up to the 5 gallon/40 pint mark with cold water.

- Wash your hands and arms and stir the wort. Make sure you get right to the bottom and get all the clumps dissolved. This is worth doing near to a sink and to leave the tap running so you can wash up without too much mess. Also, you can aerate the wort whilst stirring, which helps the yeast to start quickly.

- Stir the yeast and, making sure it's all dissolved in the water and pour it into the bucket. Stir and aerate again.

- *This is the time to measure the Original Gravity*

- Put the lid on the bucket. I usually seal it down then just crack one corner open and drape a towel over. This gives the CO_2 somewhere to escape and ensures no bugs can enter. If the lid is fully sealed, the pressure will build up and find its way out the weakest point (the lid) but it could be messy.

- Put the bucket into your designated fermenting area and leave for about a week.

After a couple of days, you should see some serious yeast action in the form of a 'krausen' on the top, a large, frothy yeast pancake. This will die down after a while.

After a week or so, check that there are no more bubbles rising to the surface. If there are, leave it a while longer.

- *This would be the time to check the Final gravity. Recommended if you're bottling the beer!!*

Once you are completely satisfied that fermentation has finished, or your hydrometer reading has been the same for three days in a row, it's time to transfer your beer into bottles or barrel.

Have your sanitised and sterilised syphon tube at the ready, along with either 40 bottles and caps, or pressure barrel, all sterilised and rinsed.

You will need to prime the bottles or barrel to give it 'fizz'. Half a teaspoon is a good start for each 500ml bottle, less if using smaller bottles. **DO NOT** be tempted to over prime bottles as, once pressure has built up, they will become glass bombs. Messy and potentially dangerous. I usually measure out the amount for each bottle (somewhere between 3 and 4 grams per bottle depending on type of beer and level of carbonation needed). 70 to 85 grams will be fine for a barrel.

Plonk the end of the syphon tube (end without the tap) in the beer, making sure that it's not touching the bottom as you don't want to suck up all the sediment. It's sometimes best to secure the tube to the side of the bucket with clothes pegs to stop it falling out and spilling beer all over your head.

Suck on the other end and place it in a bottle or the barrel and either;

- Fill the barrel and secure the lid.

- Repeat for each bottle. Crown cap each bottle and give each a small, gentle shake to dissolve the sugar.

This step needs to be done without aerating the beer. Aeration is needed when the yeast has first been pitched as the oxygen will help it to do its job. If fermentation doesn't start (it usually starts in a day or two), then give the beer another good stir and introduce more oxygen. Once the beer has finished, aeration will ruin it by causing oxidation, which will give a horrible wet cardboard flavour. Treat everything gently once you're past the first stage, don't splash the beer into the fermenter when syphoning and be careful when moving the fermenting vessel full of beer.

Place your beer barrel or bottles in a warm place (same as where it was fermented) for a week, then move to a cool place. The garage or shed floor will do. This will enable the beer to clear and condition.

This is the hard part. Waiting. It's best to wait for another week (at least) until drinking commences as your beer may not taste at its best before this. Even better, wait for 2 or 3 weeks to start drinking it as your beer will definitely taste better. It will be fine if drunk early, it certainly won't harm you, but you are not doing it justice and may think you've wasted your time making it when it doesn't taste like you hoped it would.

Leave it alone, it will be well worth it!

How To Brew All Grain Beer

We already know that there are four ingredients in beer – Water, Malt, Hops and Yeast. So which of these give beer its flavour?

The Malt

This plays a big part in providing the malty 'backbone' of a beer. The body, 'mouth feel' and colour all come from the malt. The main ingredient in most beers is pale ale or Maris Otter malt. This can be used alone to make a decent beer, or other malts can be added to this to provide different flavours and colours. Chocolate malt will give a chocolate or coffee taste and give the beer a dark colour (like a stout, for example). Biscuit malt will give the beer a biscuit or bread like taste or aroma. Caramalt can give a caramel or toffee flavour.

Torrified wheat won't add much to the flavour or colour, but will give the beer a longer-lasting head. There are many different malt types, all imparting something different on your beer. They can be used in almost infinite combinations, half the fun is experimenting with your own recipes. I always buy malt fresh and ready crushed to order.

The Hops

Hops add flavour and aroma as well as helping to preserve the beer, and will, ideally, compliment the grains. You can buy hops in pellet or leaf form, as well as hop aroma oils. I only ever buy leaf hops and always make sure they are fresh and well-sealed. Again, there are many different flavours of hops from the spiciness of Challenger, the Marmalade/orange of First Gold, and the citrus 'zing' of American hops like Citra and Cascade. Some hops are better for bittering, others for aroma, many are good for both. Again, trial and error has never been more fun!

The Yeast

Have a look at the selection of yeast available for homebrewers today. Anything from English ale yeast, American ale yeast, Belgian yeast, Kolsch ale yeast, to specific yeast strains from commercial breweries, this list is (almost) endless. Again, most of them will all impart some flavour or another. Some are invisible and can't be tasted, which is good for subtle beers or for when you want to bring out the hop and malt flavours. Others are very upfront and will give off an array of flavours and this can differ depending on which hops and malts are used. Yeast comes in dry or liquid form. Dry is easier to work with for the beginner, so liquid can wait for a couple of brews down the line.

The Process

There are 4 main processes in making all grain beer;

1 – The Mash

2 – The Sparge

3 – The Boil

4 – The Fermentation

1 – The Mash

In simple terms, this is to soak the grains in water of a certain temperature to dissolve all of the sugars. With all grain brewing, there is no need to add sugar or spraymalt, as all the sugars can be gained from the malted barley, though some brewers do add extra sugar to increase the alcohol content without adding to the grain bill (sometimes for cheapness, sometimes to produce a very thin, light beer). The more malt you use, the more sugar you'll end up with, the more the yeast has to work with, the stronger the beer will be. The mash process usually takes 90 minutes.

2 – The Sparge

To sparge is to rinse the grains, taking all those lovely sugars with the water into your boiler. This is a simple process that, if done correctly, will remove all the remaining sugars from the grains. There are many methods used for the sparge process from sparge arms to pumps, but my chosen tool for this process is a Pyrex measuring jug. I simply fill the jug with hot water, and gently pour it onto the grains without disturbing the grain bed. I did experiment with using a colander once, pouring the sparge water through it whilst resting it just above the grain bed (see pic below) but it didn't make much difference so I went back to just using the jug. The grain bed acts as a filter, filtering out the husks and stopping them from ending up in the boil. They won't do any harm but the clearer the wort, the better.

You can see that the grain bed is about an inch below the water level. The tap to the right is open and running slowly, and the sparge water is added at the same rate as this so the bed doesn't dry out but also making sure that the water doesn't get too deep above the grain

A Rolling Boil

3 – The Boil

The boiling of the collected wort for either 60 or 90 minutes. Hops are added to the boil to give the beer bitterness, flavour and aroma, and the oils help to preserve the beer. Bittering hops are usually added at the start of the boil and aroma hops are added with 10 or 15 minutes to go and sometimes at 'flame out' (exactly what is says, when you turn the heat off). The addition of hops at the 10 or 15 minute mark will also add some bittering to the beer, but a lot less than they would if boiled for longer.

After the boil, the wort is cooled to around 20°C. This is best done as quickly as possible as, the quicker the yeast is pitched, the less chance of an infection getting in and spoiling your beer. Some brewers don't use any kind of cooler, preferring instead to wait for the beer to naturally cool. Given the temperatures involved, this can take several hours or even overnight.

4 – The Ferment

It is then just a case of transferring the cooled wort to your fermenting bin, pitching the yeast, and proceeding exactly the same as with a kit.

The process of brewing all grain beer is not dissimilar to that of making kit beer, only with a kit the hard work has been done for you. The grains have been mashed, sparged, hopped, boiled and condensed down into a nice, easy-to-use tin that you just have to add water and sugar to.

On top of the equipment you already have for making kit beer, you will need;

Hot Liquor Tun

Mash Tun

Boiler (can also double as a HLT)

Wort Chiller (optional)

*Top:HLT/Boiler Middle:Mash Tun
Bottom:Fermenting bucket*

Hot Liquor Tun

This is used to heat the water (known as liquor in brewing terminology) to the correct temperature before adding it to the mash tun. It will then be used to heat the sparge water. The HLT can be either plastic or stainless steel with an electric element or a gas burner underneath.

Mash Tun

Where the mash takes place. This should ideally hold around 30 litres as the mash water and grains take up a lot of space, especially for bigger beers or those with a complex grain recipe (grain bill). It should also be insulated as the mash needs to stay at a constant temperature for 90 minutes. Some mash tuns have an element which will keep the water at the right temperature, others can be wrapped in sleeping bags or duvets to hold the heat in. My mash tun is a 30 litre cool box complete with a tap. It keeps the grains at an even temperature for 90 minutes and came with a built in strainer which stop the grains from entering the tap, which would cause a blockage, whilst allowing the wort to flow freely.

Boiler

This needs to hold a rolling boil for 60 or 90 minutes. Electric elements can burn out or the thermostat will keep cutting in and out, thus losing the boil. Some brewers prefer gas for this reason. The boiler will also need a tap and it is useful to try and get a hop strainer fitted too. I don't have any form of strainer and, on occasion, hops will block my tap and stop the liquid from flowing. I get round this by having my trusty jug sterilised ready to transfer the wort by hand.

My boiler also doubles as my HLT thus saving quite a bit of money and saving space. The only difference is that I have to collect all my wort in fermenting buckets before I can start the boil, whereas with a separate boiler and HLT I could sparge straight into the boiler. I have never found this to be a problem though so will stick with this system for now.

Wort Chiller

There are a few different ways of chilling your wort down to 'pitching' temperature. If the wort is too hot, the yeast will be instantly killed. Getting the wort down to around 20° is not easy, even with the use of a cooler, especially in summer.

My wort chiller is a copper coil which has an inlet and an outlet hose fitted. The inlet is connected to a cold tap, the outlet put down the drain. When the boil has 10 minutes to go, I drop the coil into the boiling wort to sterilise it (having rinsed it first). It is advisable to have the inlet connected to the tap before doing this as any cold water left in the hose, now heated, can start to spit out of the end of the hose. Once the boil has finished I simply turn on the cold tap and wait. It can take anywhere between 20 and 35 minutes to cool down 23 litres.

Wort Chiller…

…in action

PRE-BREW

You will need to measure your boiler, HLT and mash tun deadspace – this is the liquid left in the bottom of the vessel below the level of the tap outlet.

Put a good few gallons of water in both your mash tun, HLT and boiler, making sure the level is above the tap outlet. Empty each vessel using the tap. When nothing more comes out of the tap, there will still be that liquid left in the bottom of the vessel. Measure this deadspace and make a note of it somewhere and keep it safe.

This is important to do before you start brewing, I would recommend you measure these volumes a few days before instead of the morning of your first brew day. They will only need to be measured once.

Test Your Gear

It is often a good idea to test, or 'dry run' your new equipment, just to check that everything works OK and there are no issues or leaks. These will be easier to fix and a lot cheaper if there is an issue when full of hot water, rather than expensive grains or beer, which may have to be wasted. Also, make sure your boiler can hold a rolling boil for a while. It would be a good time to measure your 'boil off' rate too, otherwise known as evaporation. Most boilers will lose about 1 to 1.5 litres per hour of boil, but some can be as high as 2.5 litres per hour, depending on the shape and size.

Some people measure and record the time it takes for the water to heat (for mashing/sparging) and the time it takes to reach a boil. It is surprising, and will often catch a new brewer out, how long it takes for some equipment to reach the required temperature. For instance, my boiler takes about 40 to 50 minutes to reach a boil, and that is using wort straight from the sparge, i.e. it's already hot.

Still, all the waiting leaves plenty of time to measure grain and hops, clean up, or have a cup of tea.

Water Volume

OK, so we need 23 litres (40 pints) in the fermenter, at the end of the process.

We will have to account for the following losses;

Deadspace - Boiler/HLT/Mash Tun

Grains – They soak up about their own weight in water, so 5 litres will be lost using 5kg of grain

Boil – This will depend on your equipment but somewhere between 1 and 1.5 litres an hour

Hops – Another litre soaked up

Cooling – A litre will be lost when the liquid shrinks

The sum is as follows;

Amount of beer required + deadspace + grain loss + boil loss + hops loss + cooling loss = amount of liquor needed to start with.

My equipment would need;

23 litres + 5 (grain) + 3 (deadspace) + 1 (hops) + 1 (cooling) + 2 (boil)

= 35 litres*

using 5 kg of grain and boiling for 90 minutes

The best way, I have found, to work all this out is using a computer programme designed for the purpose. I personally use Beersmith, but there are many other good ones available, either free or for a small price. You can enter all your losses and it will account for the amount of grain you are using (which will generally differ from batch to batch). You can set up a profile for your equipment and it will take your losses into account for every recipe and tell you exactly how much liquor you will need for the mash and sparge, plus the temperature it will need to be heated to.

It saves a lot of time and calculations!

Let's Brew Some AG

Recipe

You will need to formulate a recipe and buy some malt, hops and yeast from your local homebrew shop (preferably, support local if you can) or online retailer.

For the purposes of this easy recipe, you will need the following;

5kg Pale Ale Malt

100g Challenger Hops*

1 sachet S04 dried English ale yeast

This recipe will only use one hop variety for ease, but your future brews can use more. You won't need the whole 100g, but that is the smallest size you can buy. Wrap the rest up tightly and stick them in the freezer, they will last a while until the next time you need them

I'm assuming by now that you have grasped the basic process of keeping everything clean and sanitised? Good, I won't need to add those steps in this time.

The first thing we need to do is to heat some water for the mash. This will depend on how much grain you are using and what temperature mash you are aiming for. I will explain this in more detail in a later chapter but, for now, we are using 5kg grain and we are aiming for a 66° mash.

- Heat up your mash water. In my case, for this recipe, it's 13.04 litres at 75.7° Celsius (call it 76°)*

*The grains are cool and will cool the water down so this figure, known as the 'strike temperature', is always higher, usually around 10 degrees higher than the required mash temperature, to account for this

- *You may want to pre-heat your mash tun using boiled water from the kettle. Empty this out before proceeding to the next step.*

- Once heated, turn your HLT tap on and let the water flow into your mash tun and, at the same time, slowly pour the 5kg of pale malt in. Do this slowly and stir as you go. Small lumps, or dough balls, may appear but these can (and must) be dispersed and mixed in. You can do this by using a large spoon or spatula and squashing it against the side of the tun.

- Give it a good mix and check the temperature. It should be at 66°. If higher, stir the mixture for a minute or two until it lowers. If too low, boil the kettle and add water until it reaches 66°.

Don't panic with this step. Get the mash on and leave it alone for 10 minutes or so with the lid on. The temperature may even out. If you start adjusting the temperature too early, it can swing up and down and be confusing, so it is best to wait. Also, be aware that the temperature within the mash tun can fluctuate from end to end and top to bottom. You can check the mash periodically with your thermometer but, every time you open the lid, heat will be lost. I use a probe* thermometer and leave it in the tun for the duration of the mash and, depending on where I place the probe, the temperature can be as much as 2° different so, before measuring, give the grains a gentle stir.

* It is best to buy a thermometer that has a 'probe' fitted so the wire can be run under the lid. The temperature will be displayed on a digital readout that can be checked easily at a glance without going near the mash tun.

- Secure the lid and leave for 90 minutes

- *Meanwhile, measure out your sparge water. Mine would be 24.17 litres. Heat this to 75.6°.*

- Prepare a bucket to catch the wort in.

I use 2 so I only have to half fill each and not lift a full bucket up high to fill the boiler. The boiler will still be half full of sparge water at this point so obviously the wort can't be added to it just yet until the sparge is finished*

*Ignore this if you're using a separate HLT and boiler

- When the 90 minutes are up, slowly open the tap of the mash tun to just more than a trickle and catch the wort in a measuring jug. Fill this and return it, slowly and gently, to the mash. This is called the first runnings and what you are trying to achieve is for the wort to flow clear. You will notice that the first runnings is full of husks and debris. Once you have done this a few times, it will start to clear, which means that the grain is forming a natural filter bed.

First Runnings: Note bits of floating grains and husks

Second Runnings; this is what you are aiming for

- Once the wort runs clear, you can now let it flow into your bucket. You now need to keep about an inch of liquid on top of the grain bed to stop it from drying out. Do this using the sparge water. Fill the jug up and pour it, again gently, onto the grain. I run some gently down the sides of the mash tun and some slowly over the rest of the bed, pouring from as low as I can get. The basic idea is to keep the temperature even across the whole of the mash tun whilst not disturbing the bed.

- This process can take up to 45 minutes but, the slower it is done, the more sugars you will collect from the malt, and the less chance there is of a stuck mash*

If you are unlucky enough to get a stuck mash, close the tap of the mash tun to a trickle, stir the grains until the liquor starts to flow from the tap and repeat the process of collecting the first runnings. Generally, a stuck mash is due to either running the liquor through the tap too quickly or disturbing the grain bed with the sparge water, though some speciality grains will increase the chance of a stuck mash.

- Once the sparge is complete, pour the wort into your boiler. Take a hydrometer reading to find out the pre-boil gravity,

- *Meanwhile, measure out your hops; 40g (for bittering) and 20g (for aroma)*

🍺 When the rolling boil is reached, add 40g of hops

🍺 *Meanwhile, clean your mash tun out for next time, and get your fermenter sterilised ready for use*

🍺 At the 1 hour and 15 minutes point of the boil, add the 20g of hops

🍺 *If you are using a wort cooler, add it to the boil (after rinsing) with 10 minutes to go, this will sterilise it*

- At the 90 minute point, switch the heat off (and turn the cold water tap on if using a cooler)

- *Meanwhile, boil some water in the kettle, add it to a mug, wait for it to cool to room temperature, and sprinkle the dried yeast on top.*

Rehydrating the yeast - The instructions say to sprinkle the dry yeast straight onto the wort but I, like many other brewers, prefer to rehydrate first

- Once the temperature has reached 20°, open the tap and let the wort splash into the fermenter. The aeration won't hurt it as it will aid the yeast in starting.

- *It is handy to use some form of strainer to stop all the small bits of hops from entering the fermenter. I use a sieve for this purpose.*

- Grab a sample at this point to check the original gravity

- Once in the fermenter, pitch the yeast (having stirred it in the mug to make sure there are no lumps or dry bits)

- Clean up so everything is ready for next time

So there it is, after a week's wait you will have made beer. If you did it correctly, it will be better than most beers you can buy either in the supermarket or pub.

A Word About 'Efficiency'

You will need to find out what your efficiency is. It's easy to figure out using Beersmith and other software, and it will be necessary to make beer of a consistent strength. The original recipe called for 5kg pale ale malt and this will give a different beer strength depending on your efficiency. With an efficiency of 92%, 5kg of malt will produce beer of 5.5%. If your efficiency is lower, at 72% for example, the same amount of malt will yield an ABV of 4.3%. Quite a difference, huh? That slow mashing process may be boring, but the better you do it, the higher your efficiency should be. Mine is consistent for now, so I know exactly how much malt to use to give me the percentage I want from my finished beer. Also, it goes without saying that the higher your efficiency is, the cheaper your beer will be. Most of my beers come in around 40p to 50p a pint, depending on the strength and how many hops I use, but some have been lower. This is the equivalent to the price of a kit beer (either all extract or using spraymalt) and, although it takes more work to make an AG beer, I think it's well worth the extra effort!

Mash Temperature And Its Effect On Attenuation

I won't delve too deeply into this subject as it is a lot more complicated than I can explain but the basic principal is quite easy to grasp. It's all down to what effect the temperature has on the grains and how much usable sugar you can obtain in your mash.

Our all grain beer was mashed at 66°. If we were to have mashed at 65° or 64°, we would have made a dry, lighter bodied beer.

If we had mashed at 67° or 68°, we could have made a bigger bodied beer, but slightly sweeter. This is due to more unfermentable sugars being released from the grains with the higher temperature.

The dry beer would have attenuated quite low, to say 1.006 whereas the bigger beer may have attenuated to 1.012 or higher. Our 66 degree beer will probably finish around the 1.010 mark.

It's quite hard to work out, as a beginner, where your beer will finish up. If you use the same yeast and same mash temperature every time, as well as the same recipe and methods, the final gravity will usually be consistent. You can probably read endless books on the subject but I have found that trial and error is the best solution to this.

How Much Does It Cost?

The cost of the equipment will, obviously, depend on what you choose to buy and where you buy it from. A stainless steel fermenter will cost a lot more than a plastic one. Whether you choose an electric or gas boiler will also have a bearing. Some electric boilers are plastic, some stainless steel, some very expensive. You may choose to buy a 30 litre stainless steel stock pot to use as a boiler but you will also need to factor in the cost of a gas ring and bottle, unless you are going to use the kitchen stove. This can be a messy solution (if you get a boil-over), and some kitchen cookers won't heat the pot to the sufficient temperature to achieve a rolling boil.

For making beers kits;

This is how much it cost me to start making beer.

King Keg Pressure barrel £45.99

Fermenting Bin £8

Beer Kit (incl yeast) £12

Spray Malt (1kg) £9.50

Total £75.49

This works out at £1.88 per pint for the first batch of 40 pints!

Subsequent batches will be around 50p a pint.

For making all grain beer;

The extra equipment cost me;

Buffalo 3KW Electric Boiler £80

Mash Tun £50

Wort Cooler £32

Misc. (includes thermometer, mixing paddle etc) £30

Total £199

Add to this another £20 for malt, hops and yeast and your first 40 pint batch will have cost £5.47 per pint. Quite expensive for a pint (though, some pubs aren't far off that now) but again, subsequent pints will cost 40p to 60p depending on how many, and which variety of, grain and hops are used.

-All prices correct as of 2014

Useful Links

Jim's Beer Kit – Online Forum

A handy online forum with lots of good advice and recipe ideas

http://www.jimsbeerkit.co.uk

Brew Your Own – A How-To Homebrew Beer Magazine

A monthly magazine for homebrewers. The website also contains some excellent articles and beer style guides

http://byo.com

The Malt Miller – Online Shop

For malt, hops, yeast, and any other ingredients you'll need for beer

http://www.themaltmiller.co.uk

Hop List – Online Hop Resource

Everything you could ever wish to know about hops. Includes flavour, aroma, and which beers each variety is most suited to

http://www.hopslist.com

Leyland Homebrew – Online Equipment Supplier

One of the many excellent suppliers of beer kits, bottling equipment, beer starter kits, kegs and ingredients on the internet

http://www.leylandhomebrew.com

BeerSmith – Brewing Software

Easy to use program for calculating recipes, water volume, temperature and much more. Free trial for 30 days

http://www.beersmith.com

Also from the author

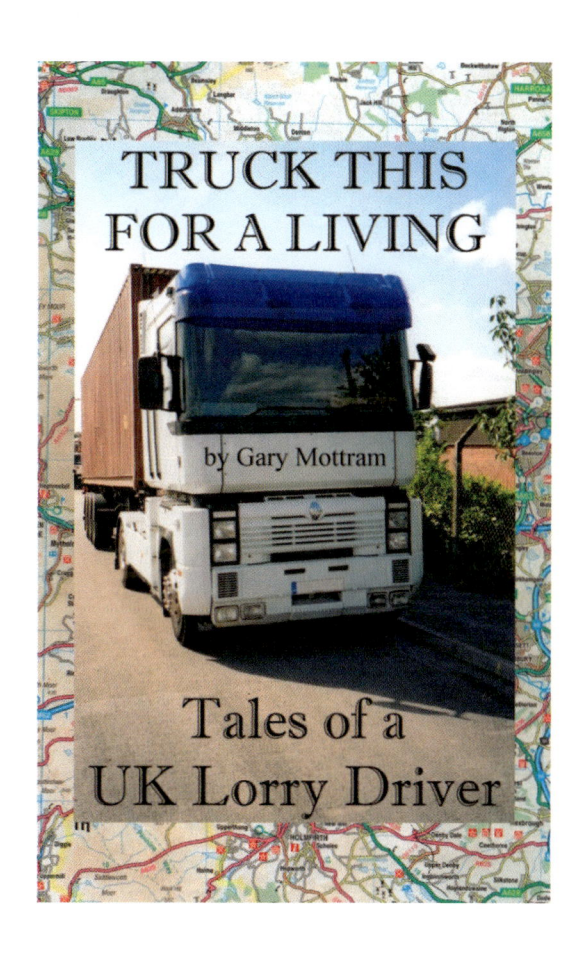

OUT NOW ON KINDLE & PAPERBACK

Available from Amazon

Printed in Great Britain
by Amazon